Y0-BDD-103

F
582
H

Hutchins, Ross E

Lives of an oak tree

C I

DATE DUE

4	8PD	32
JUN 5	DEC 15 1981	MAY 0 7 1982
6	8PD	24
Jun 3 75	JAN 5 1982	Oct 15
T6		25
Barbara T36		NOV 1 2 1998
8PD	25	
DEC 1 1981	APR 1 7 1991	
8PD		
DEC 8 1981		

Life cycle of an oak tree from sprouting of the acorn until it falls in a storm 300 years later. Will be interesting especially after a hike in the woods.

by ROSS E. HUTCHINS

Illustrated by Jerome P. Connolly

LIVES
OF AN
OAK TREE

RAND McNALLY & COMPANY
CHICAGO · NEW YORK · SAN FRANCISCO

GALINAS SCHOOL
North San Pedro Road
San Rafael, Calif.

AUTHOR'S NOTE

In America there are many kinds of oak trees. They range from the small scrub oaks of the West to the stately oaks of the East. Our story could easily be about almost any of these trees, from a live oak, spreading its great branches beside a lazy southern bayou, to a red oak with its crimson leaves adding color to the autumn woods of northern mountains. Actually, I had the graceful white oak in mind as the central figure of the story. These trees grow almost everywhere in the East, sometimes reaching a diameter of 8 feet and an age of nearly 500 years. They have been called the kings of the eastern forests.

Another "character" in this story is the cottonwood, a tree belonging to the poplar and willow family. These trees often grow to a height of 100 feet in 15 years. In May they shed their tiny seeds, each with its attached bit of down or "cotton." The cottonwoods grow almost everywhere in America including river banks of the arid Southwest where they received their Spanish name *álamo*.

Copyright © 1962 by Rand McNally & Company
Copyright 1962 under International Copyright
    Union by Rand McNally & Company
All rights reserved   Printed in U.S.A.
Library of Congress Catalog Card Number: 62-12649
Third printing, 1965

Once upon a time there was an old oak tree. It spread its branches beside a great river.

Each spring the oak tree clothed itself with green leaves.

When summer came, many seeds grew on its twigs. Each seed was green and fitted with a pretty cap.

We call these seeds acorns.

In autumn, the acorns turned brown.

Squirrels climbed to the tallest branches of the oak tree and cut the acorns off.
They carried them down and buried them deep in the ground.

In winter, when they were hungry, the squirrels dug up the acorns and ate them.

The acorns were very bitter, but the squirrels did not mind.

One acorn was buried very deep, and the squirrels forgot where it was.

Snow made a white blanket on the ground, and kept the acorn covered all winter.

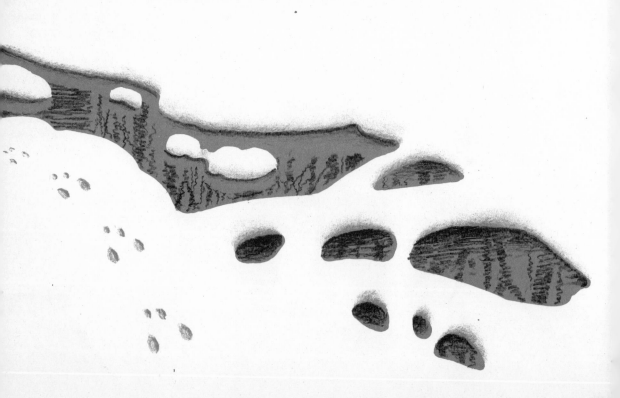

At last spring came and melted the snow, and the sun warmed the earth.

The buried acorn felt the warmth and began to grow. It sent up a stem with two green leaves. It also sent a rootlet down into the earth.

This was the beginning of another oak tree.

All summer the little oak tree grew.
The big old oak tree shaded it from
the sun.

Beetles found the tiny oak tree and
chewed pieces out of its tender young
leaves.

But sharp-eyed birds saw the beetles
and ate them, before they could hurt
all of the leaves.

One evening a mother deer and her
spotted fawn lay down to rest under
the large oak.

The little oak was crushed to the
earth.

For many days it lay flat upon the
ground.

Then came a summer shower, and the moisture soaked into the earth.

The little oak liked the moisture.

It began to straighten up, and its leaves reached up to the light again.

Soon it was as good as new.

Summer turned to autumn once more,
and the days grew short.

One morning it was winter; the oak
leaves were covered with frost.
The squirrels were busy gathering
acorns again, but the little oak had
none, so they paid no attention to it.

Slowly the little oak grew.
Ever so slowly its tender roots pushed through the soil.

Tiny tubes inside the roots and stems carried water
and other good things from the earth up to the leaves.

The leaves of the oak were like green factories.
They breathed in gas from the air, and drank the water
that came from the soil. These they put together to make
food for the growing tree. This food was carried to the
other parts of the tree by tiny tubes that ran downward
from the leaves.

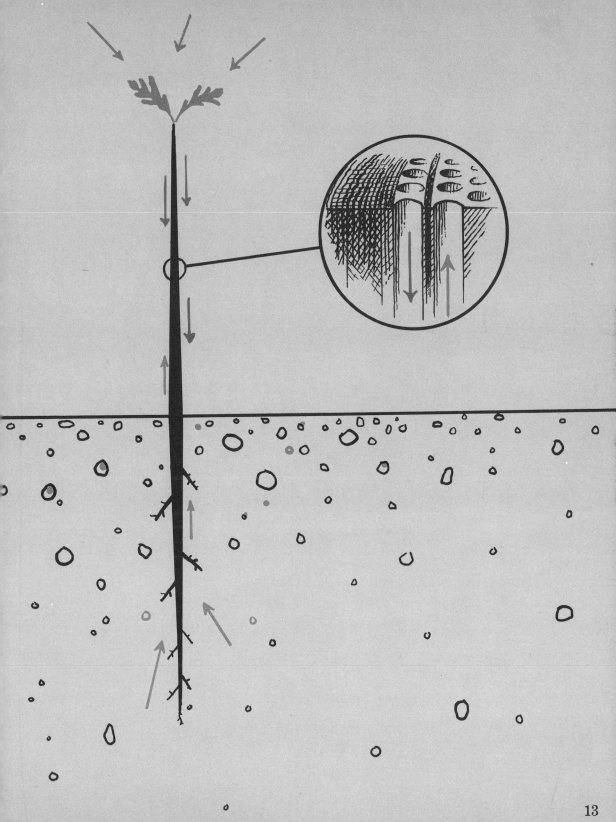

Year by year the roots pushed deeper and deeper into the soil.

The growing tree needed long roots to anchor it against the wind.

As the oak slowly grew larger it also needed more water and food.

Many years passed and the oak became a full-grown tree. It spread its branches out over the river and towered above the other forest trees.

One spring a pair of robins came.

Like many other birds they had flown south in the autumn, and had stayed away all winter.

But now it was spring and they came back again to build a nest in the oak.

They gathered moss and twigs which they carefully wove together.

The nest was finished just in time to hold the four blue eggs the mother robin laid.

The robins were very proud of the eggs.

The mother robin sat on the eggs all day to keep them warm.

And the father robin sat on a high branch of the oak and sang to her.

GALLINAS SCHOOL
North San Pedro Road
San Rafael, Calif.

17

At last one day the eggs began to hatch.

First there were cracks in each blue egg; then the baby robins appeared.

The parents were very excited.

They flew down to the ground and hunted for worms to feed to the little birds.

One day a hawk chased father robin, but he hid in the
oak tree and escaped.

The four little robins grew quickly.
When they were full grown they left the nest, and the parent robins gave them flying lessons.

When autumn came they all flew south again for the winter.
The oak tree was left alone.

21

More years passed, and the oak tree kept on growing.

Its limbs were covered with mosses and ferns, and some were as thick as a man's waist.

In one of the larger branches was a big hole.

A family of raccoons found the hole, and decided it would be a good place to live.

There was room enough for all of the raccoons inside.

During the day they slept in their dark, cozy home.

At night, when the moon hung over the river, the raccoons climbed down to the ground.

They searched in the river for frogs and crayfish.

The river flowed softly in the moonlight, and the raccoons moved like shadows along the edge.

High up in the oak sat a great horned
owl. It hooted very loudly, but the raccoons were not afraid. They went right
on catching frogs and crayfish.

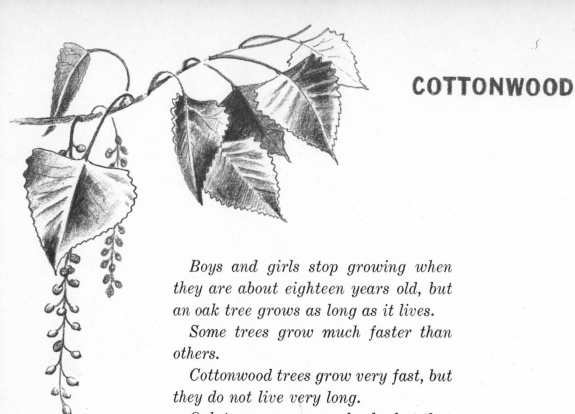

COTTONWOOD

Boys and girls stop growing when they are about eighteen years old, but an oak tree grows as long as it lives.

Some trees grow much faster than others.

Cottonwood trees grow very fast, but they do not live very long.

Oak trees grow very slowly, but they may live for three hundred years.

Each spring they add a new growth layer under their bark. This is called a "growth ring."

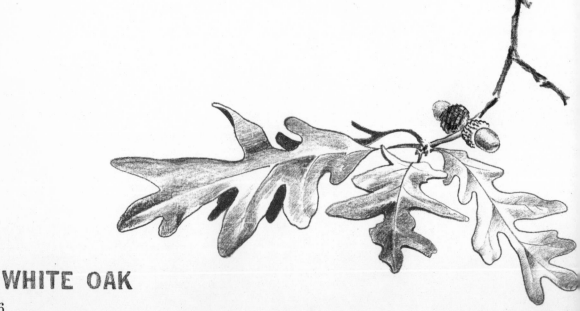

WHITE OAK

You can tell how old a tree is by counting its growth rings.

The next time you are in the woods, find a tree stump. Count the rings of yearly growth on its top. This will tell you how old the tree was when it was cut down.

You can also see these growth rings in the end of a stick of firewood.

On a summer day, when our oak was
a hundred years old, a storm came.

Torrents of rain fell, and out of the
sky came a bolt of lightning.

The lightning struck one of the large
limbs of the oak, and the limb came
crashing to the ground.

A few days later a man came with his team of horses.
He chopped the great limb up with his ax.
Then he hauled the pieces away in his wagon.
He thought it would make good firewood.

Another winter came and all the trees were bare.
The ground was covered with snow, and the river was
frozen over.

In early spring the snow and ice started to melt.
Then there was rain.
It rained for many days.
The raccoons and the squirrels stayed in their tree
home, curled up and dry.

Soon the great river began to rise. It flowed over its banks, and covered the forest with water.

All the creatures who lived on the ground in the forest hurried to find a place that was dry.

The roots of the great oak had grown and spread for some distance under the soil. These roots held the soil and kept it from washing away during times of flood.

Slowly, as time passed, the ground near the oak became higher and higher. Now it was so high that flood waters never flowed over it.

The forest dwellers were afraid of the rising waters. They remembered the high ground around the oak tree, and knew they would be safe there.

Rabbits with wet fur came splashing through the forest, and two deer came wading through the water.

Foxes and wildcats came out of their hiding places.

All the animals hurried toward the high ground. The wildcats climbed up on a high limb of the oak tree.

For many days the animals stayed under the spreading oak while brown waters rushed past.

Each day they watched big trees float by.

Many of the trees had creatures like themselves clinging to them.

At last the great river returned to its bed, and the animals could leave their safe, dry place under the oak and hunt for food.

In a time of need the oak tree had given shelter to the wild creatures of the forest.

Summer came and went and again it was autumn.

The birds, and the flock of ducks and geese were winging their way southward.

The stars were bright during the crisp autumn nights.

A ground hog had dug its den under a root of the great oak. All summer it had fed upon grass and become fat.

Now, with the coming of late autumn, it curled up in its snug den and went to sleep. It would sleep away the cold months of winter.

When spring came it would wake up and feed upon the fresh grass.

The leaves of the oak tree had now changed from green to orange and gold.

As the days passed, the colorful oak leaves began to fall, one by one.

Soon the ground beneath the tree was carpeted with golden leaves that rustled in the autumn breezes.

Slowly, as the months passed, the leaves rotted.

These rotted leaves fed the roots of the oak, and would help to grow more leaves the next year.

The oak was very old now.

For nearly three hundred springs, it had grown new leaves.

For the same number of autumns its leaves had turned golden and then fallen.

It had been growing there for longer than any man could remember.

Year by year the oak had grown ever larger.

Its great moss-covered limbs now extended far out over the river.

No tree in the forest was older or larger.

Most of the great forest had been cut down.

Fields of corn grew where the cool, green forest had been.

In the air above the oak there had once been only eagles.

Now great silvery airplanes streaked across the sky.

The world about the oak had slowly changed.

But the oak had changed, too.

Many of its great limbs were dead.

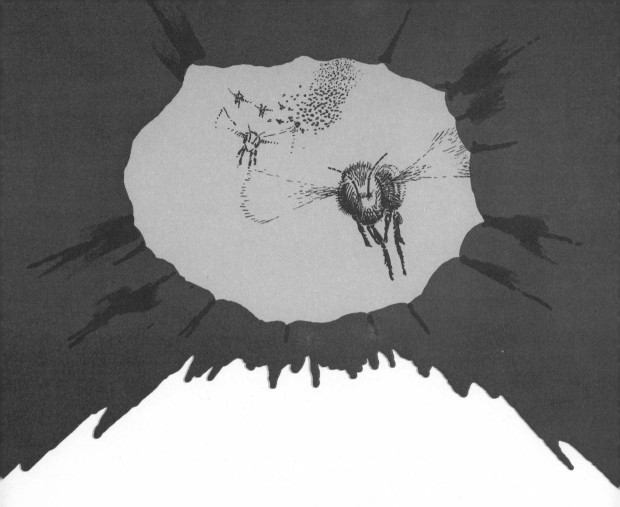

One warm spring day a great swarm of honeybees came to the oak.

They had sent out scout bees the day before.

The scouts had found a knothole high in the oak, and now the scouts led the swarm into the knothole.

In the swarm there were a queen bee and thousands of worker honeybees.

The bees all went to work, and soon there were layers of wax honeycomb.

These layers were made up of hundreds of neat, six-sided cells.

The worker bees flew away and found flowers blooming in the nearby fields.

They gathered nectar and pollen from the flowers that they carried back to the nest in the great oak.

The bees worked hard for many days, and soon the wax cells were filled.

There were young bees in some of the cells, and honey and pollen in others.

The bees had made the honey out of the nectar they had gathered from the flowers.

By autumn they had a large store of golden honey, and were ready for a long winter.

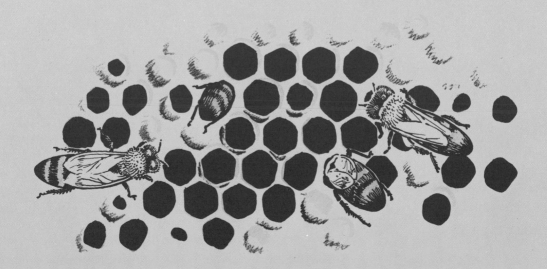

When spring came again, most of the forest trees had new, fresh green leaves.

But the limbs of our oak were bare.

After three hundred years of living, the huge tree was dead. Sap no longer flowed up and down its trunk and branches. Its roots no longer pushed their slow way through the soil.

High up in the tree the honeybees were building more comb.

Farther up the trunk a woodpecker family was hammering a hole in the wood to make a nest. All day they drove their sharp beaks into the wood.

The sound of their hammering could be heard far away.

Chips of the wood fell to the ground.

After many days of work the nest hole was deep enough.

The mother woodpecker laid four white eggs in the nest, and sat on them.

Sometimes she left the nest and flew away to hunt for food.

The woodpeckers didn't need leaves on the tree because their hole was so deep.

But no songbirds built nests in the dead oak this spring. They needed trees with lots of leaves that would hide their nests from enemies.

The squirrels, too, moved away to another oak tree. They needed a living tree with buds in spring and acorns in autumn.

Summer passed, and winter came again.

The bare limbs of the oak still towered above the smaller trees of the forest.

A red-tail hawk used one of the highest limbs for
a perch. He could see a long way in every direction.

Sometimes he would spot rats and mice on the
ground.

Then he would drop down on outspread wings and
catch the creatures in his claws.

With spring came warm rains.
The water soaked into the oak.
Pieces of bark fell away, leaving the
bare wood.

Pretty green beetles came and laid their eggs.
The eggs hatched into white, caterpillar-like grubs that
bored through the softening wood.

This softened the wood even more.

Then came molds that grew like fur upon the decaying wood.

The molds were of many colors and they dusted the bark with millions of their tiny "seeds."

These "seeds" or spores tinted the bark with the hues of the rainbow.

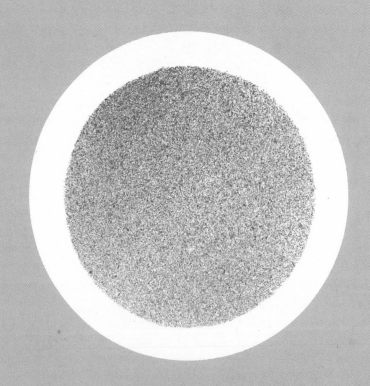

Within the thick wood of the oak were hundreds of different kinds of boring insects.

Woodpeckers came and sat on the bare limbs and listened to the borers working deep inside the tree.

They drilled into the burrows and speared the insects with their long, sharp tongues.

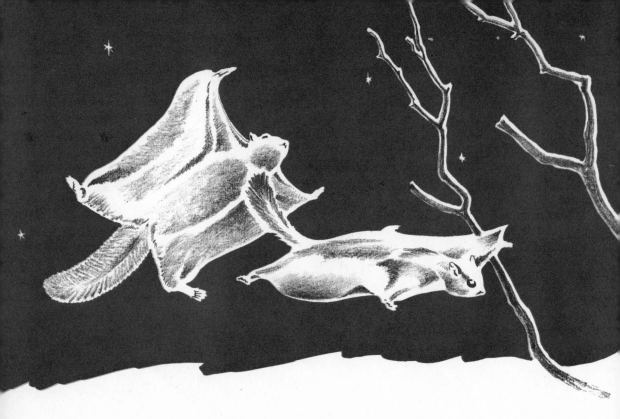

One autumn day a pair of soft and furry flying squirrels saw the dead oak.

They had been living in another tree a short distance
away, but they thought the dead oak tree would make a
better home. So they spread their legs and hopped off the
tree where they were.

Between their front and back legs they had webs of
skin. On these webs they sailed through the air and
landed at the base of the oak.

The flying squirrels scrambled up the tree and climbed
all over it, looking into every hole and crack.

Finally they found what they were searching for—an
old woodpecker hole.

They gathered fine grasses near the tree and made a
warm nest.

Now they were ready for winter.

One night a great storm swept through the forest.

There were bright flashes of lightning and terrible winds.

All the forest trees bent under the force of the storm.

The flying squirrels woke up, frightened, and peeked out.

In the glow from the lightning flashes, they could see the river water being whipped into foam.

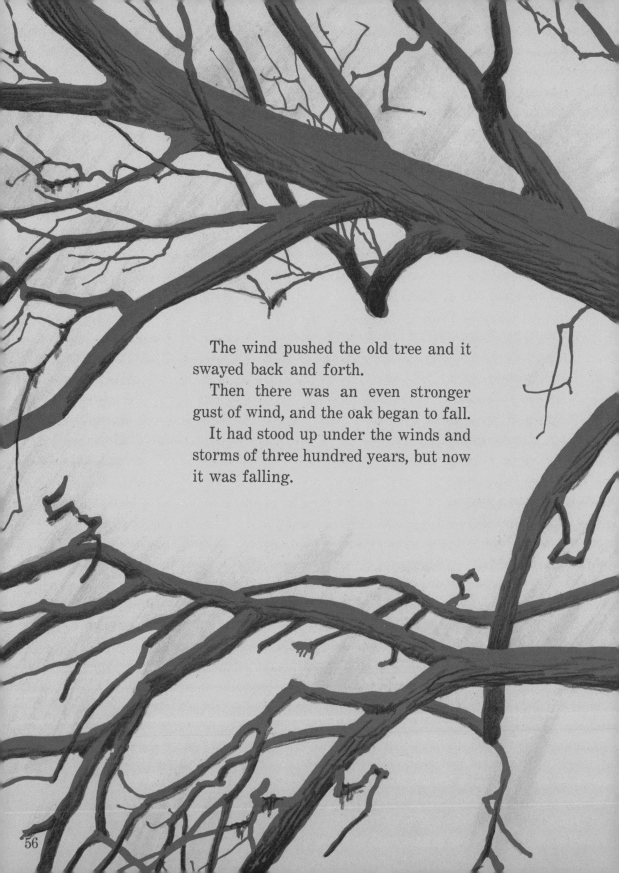

The wind pushed the old tree and it
swayed back and forth.

Then there was an even stronger
gust of wind, and the oak began to fall.

It had stood up under the winds and
storms of three hundred years, but now
it was falling.

It crashed to the ground with a sound like thunder.
The earth shook.

When the oak hit the ground, it split open, and its branches broke off.

The flying squirrels were wet and frightened.

The colony of bees was torn apart.

Honey and comb were scattered all about.

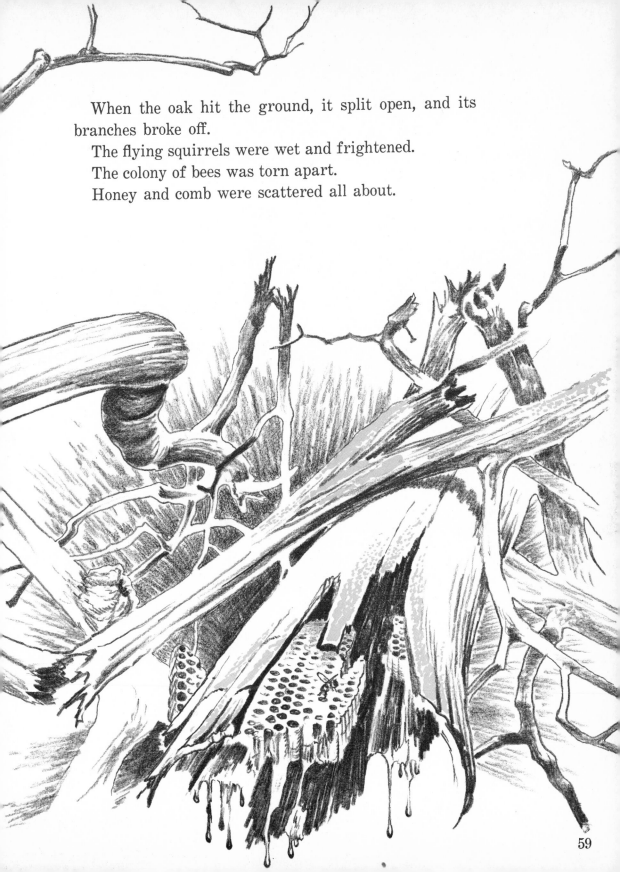

When the storm was over, the remains of the old oak
lay along the river bank.

The flying squirrels found a new den in another tree,
but the honeybees were all dead.

Soon it began to snow, and deep drifts formed over the oak.

Beneath the snow, field mice found the oak.

They explored the great trunk and found the old woodpecker holes.

Inside these holes it was warm and comfortable.

The mice made their nests there.

At night they made trips away from the tree to hunt for seeds.

When spring came, mosses slowly spread over the fallen tree like a green blanket.

Then came ferns that unfolded their fronds in graceful curves.

Field mice and shrews reared families in the dark tunnels inside the fallen tree.

Though it was no longer alive, the oak still gave shelter to many of the small creatures of the forest.

INDEX

Growth, of boys and girls, 26; of oak tree, 7, 12, 14, 15, 22, 26, 27, 42

Growth rings, 26, 27

Hawk, chasing of robin by, 19; food for, 49; and oak tree, 49

Honeybees, and oak tree, 44, 59, 60; making of honey by, 44–46

Insects, in oak tree, 53

Leaves, color of, 40, 42; eaten by beetles, 8; falling of, 40, 42; frost on, 11; making of food by, 12, 41; need of, by birds, 47; protected by birds, 8; rotting of, 41; in spring, 3, 7, 46; tubes in, 12

Lightning, and oak tree, 28, 55

Mice, as food for hawks, 49; *see also* Field mice

Molds, and oak tree, 52

Mosses, on oak tree, 22, 42, 62

Nests, field mice and, 61; hiding of, 47; raccoons and, 22; robins and, 16–20; woodpeckers and, 46

Oak tree, age of, 26, 27, 28, 42, 46; in autumn, 4, 40, 42; beetles and, 8, 51; beginning of, 7; boring insects in, 53; changing of, 43; death of, 43, 46; and deer, 9, 35; falling of, 56–59; and field mice, 61, 62; flying squirrels in, 54–55, 59, 60; food for, 12, 14, 41; and foxes, 36; groundhog under, 39; growth of, 7, 12, 14, 15, 22, 26, 27, 42; hawk perches in, 49; honeybees and, 44–46, 59, 60; horned owl in, 25; leaves of, 3, 7, 8, 11, 12, 40, 41, 42, 46; and lightning, 28, 55; molds and, 52; mosses and ferns on limbs of, 22, 42, 62; protection of animals by, 19, 31, 34–37, 39, 47, 62; and rabbits, 35; raccoons nest in, 22, 31; and rain, 10, 28, 31–32, 50; robins nest in, 16–20; roots of, 7, 12, 14, 33, 41, 46; seeds of, *see* Acorns; and shrews, 62; spreading of branches by, 3, 15, 42; in spring, 3, 7, 16, 26, 31, 46, 50, 62; squirrels and, 31, 47; and storms, 28, 55–60; in summer, 3, 8, 28; and water, 10, 12; and wildcats, 36; wind and, 14, 55, 56; in winter, 11, 30, 61; wood of, 29, 50, 51–53; woodpeckers and, 46–47, 53

Owl, horned, in oak tree, 25

Rabbits, and oak tree, 35

Raccoons, make home in oak tree, 22, 31; and owl, 25; searching for food by, 24, 25

Rain, animals and, 31–32; and oak tree, 10, 28, 31–32, 50

Rats, as food for hawks, 49

River, and forest animals, 32, 34–37; freezing of, 30; melting of ice on, 31; rising and flooding of, 32–37; in storm, 55

Robins, build nest in oak tree, 16–17; eggs of, 17–18; feeding of young by, 18; flying lessons for, 20; hawk and, 19

Roots, in earth, 7, 12, 14, 33, 46; feeding of, by leaves, 41; holding of soil by, 33; tubes in, 12; and wind, 14

Seeds, as food for field mice, 61; of oak tree, *see* Acorns

Shrews, and oak tree, 62

Snow, and acorns, 6; covers dead oak tree, 61; covers ground, 6–7, 30; melting of, 7, 31

Soil, *see* Earth

Spores, of molds, 52

Spring, and acorns, 7; animals in, 31; birds in, 16, 31; ground hog and, 39; honeybees and, 44; oak tree in, 3, 7, 16, 26, 31, 46, 50, 62; rain in, 50

Squirrels, and acorns, 4–6, 11; in oak tree, 31, 47

Stems, tubes in, 12

Storms, and oak tree, 28, 55–60

Summer, ground hog and, 39; oak tree in, 3, 8, 28

Sun, warmth of, 7, 8

Trees, during flood, 37; in storm, 55; *see also* Cottonwood *and* Oak

Water, and oak tree, 10, 12; *see also* Rain *and* River

Wildcats, and oak tree, 36

Wind, and oak tree, 14, 55, 56

Winter, birds in, 16; ground hog and, 39; oak tree in, 11, 30, 61

Worms, as food for robins, 18

Wood, of oak tree, 29, 50, 51–53

Woodpeckers, field mice use holes of, 61; flying squirrels use holes of, 54; and oak tree, 46–47, 53

PRINTED IN U.S.A.